Smart Spending

Cavendish Square
New York

Rebecca Stefoff

Published in 2015 by Cavendish Square Publishing, LLC
243 5th Avenue, Suite 136, New York, NY 10016

Library of Congress Cataloging-in-Publication Data

Stefoff, Rebecca, 1951-
Smart spending / Rebecca Stefoff.
pages cm. — (First-glance finance)
Includes index.
ISBN 978-1-50260-281-7 (hardcover) ISBN 978-1-50260-098-1 (ebook)
1. Budgets, Personal—Juvenile literature. 2. Finance, Personal—Juvenile literature. 3. Consumer education—Juvenile literature. I. Title.

HG179.S55857 2015
332.024—dc23

2014025722

Editor: Amy Hayes
Senior Copy Editor: Wendy A. Reynolds
Art Director: Jeffrey Talbot
Senior Designer: Amy Greenan
Senior Production Manager: Jennifer Ryder-Talbot
Production Editor: David McNamara
Photo Research by J8 Media

The photographs in this book are used by permission and through the courtesy of: Cover photos by Kalmatsuy/Shutterstock.com, Juan Camilo Bernal/Moment Open/Getty Images; Kalmatsuy/Shutterstock.com, 1; Lee Prince/Shutterstock.com, 5; Rich Yasick/E+/Getty Images, 7; Gen Nishino/The Image Bank/Getty Images, 11; Flirt/Superstock, 13; LHF Graphics/Shutterstock.com, 14–15; Zero Creatives/Cultura/Getty Images, 17; AP Photo/Clarke Canfield, 19; Pastushenko Taras/Shutterstock.com, 20; Jupiterimages/Stockbyte/Getty Images, 21; Noel Hendrickson/Digital Vision/Thinkstock, 22; PathDoc/Shutterstock.com, 25; Yin Yang/E+/Getty Images, 27; MJTH/Shutterstock.com, 28; Blend Images/Shutterstock.com, 31; sozaijiten/Datacraft/Getty Images, 32; © iStockphoto.com/fotofrog, 33; Paul Bradbury/Caiaimage/Getty Images, 34; John Howard/Digital Vision/Getty Images, 39; © iStockphoto.com/Steve Debenport, 41. Used throughout: Paper bills, lendy16/Shutterstock.com.

Printed in the United States of America

CONTENTS

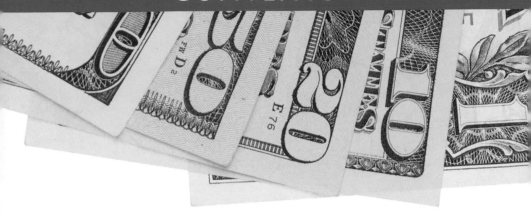

CHAPTER ONE

Buying and Selling

....

Have you ever bought something you thought you wanted, but later wished you had spent the **money** on something else? Did you ever discover that you could have bought the same thing for less money at a different store?

If this has happened to you, you're not alone. For as long as there has been money, people have made mistakes spending it. Fortunately, there are simple ways to become a smart spender and make the most of your dollars and cents.

These ancient Roman coins are made of a metal called bronze.

What Is Money?

Money is how people get paid for the work they do. They use the money they earn to pay for the things they want or need.

When you think of money, do you picture stacks of metal **coins** and piles of paper **bills**? People have used many other things for money, including seashells, cattle, and pieces of leather. Like coins and bills, these were forms of **currency**. Anything that the people of a particular country or region recognize as money is currency.

Before people agreed on what to use as currency, they **bartered**, or traded goods. A farmer might trade part of his harvest to a metalsmith in exchange for a new blade for cutting grain, for example. New kinds of currency now exist in digital form, which can be used for online spending.

Your money might be in the form of coins, bills, or digital currency. The rules of smart spending are the same for all. To start with, smart spenders know something about **advertising**. Messages that are aimed at making us want to buy things have a lot to do with the way people spend money today.

"Buy This Now!"

The word "advertising" comes from two words in Latin, the language of ancient Rome. These words are *ad vertere*. They mean, "to turn toward." Advertising is meant to catch people's attention and turn them toward whatever is being advertised.

Advertising messages, or advertisements, are usually called ads. An ad might be about a product, such as a car. It could also be about a service, such as a shop that repairs cars or a **bank** that makes **loans** to help people

The First Money

Metal coins and paper bills have been around for a long time. The oldest known coins come from China, around 1000 BCE. They were made of copper and bronze. The next place to use coins was the ancient kingdom of Lydia, in what is now Turkey. The kings of Lydia had gold and silver coins made in the seventh century BCE, more than 2,700 years ago. The Chinese also invented bills. They started printing paper money before 700 CE. Paper money didn't catch on in Europe until almost a thousand years later.

Advertising often uses loud and showy antics to grab people's attention. Ads aimed at kids are especially colorful and lively.

pay for cars. Every ad has a **sponsor**, or the person, company, or group that paid for the ad. The sponsor aims the ad at people who might become **consumers**, the ones who buy the product or use the service.

As far back as the pyramid builders of ancient Egypt, people used posters and wall paintings to advertise their goods and services. Modern advertising got its start in England around 1900, when Thomas J. Barratt pioneered new ways of promoting Pears' soap.

Two of Barratt's methods are still used by advertisers today. One method was to have famous people say good things about the soap. Barratt used scientists and opera singers as his spokespeople. Today, a spokesperson might be a movie actor or hip-hop star. Barratt's other method was to show Pears' soap in stylish homes with attractive, well-dressed people. The message was that the soap was part of a desirable lifestyle that anyone could copy.

Another advertising pioneer was Edward Bernays, who worked in the United States in the first part of the twentieth century. His approach was based on **psychology**, the study of the mind and how it works. One of his most successful methods was creating events, such as parades or contests, to draw attention to products. To advertise Ivory soap, for example, Bernays held contests for carving sculptures out of soap.

Billions of dollars are now spent each year on advertising. Ads appear in traditional places such as magazines, billboards, and television commercials. They also appear online and in social media. Ads can do more than try to sell products and services. Political candidates use them to try to win votes, or take votes away from other candidates. Public service announcements, or PSAs, are messages for the public good. Some PSAs are about the health risks of smoking or the dangers of driving after drinking alcohol.

You and Your Dollars

You and your dollars are the target of a huge advertising industry. Advertisers have special methods for drawing kids' attention to their messages. Some of those methods are:

- Cartoon characters or puppets used in commercials or as spokespeople for products
- Kids dancing, playing games, or listening to lively music while they consume a product

Are You Hungry Yet?

Fast food, sugary cereals, sugary drinks, and candy are the products most often advertised to kids during television programs. The average child sees about 4,000 of these commercials by the age of five. If you watch cartoons on Saturday morning, you could see a food ad for every five minutes of the actual TV program.

- Flashing lights and bright colors
- Online games that are sponsored by advertisers and include ads
- Videos on YouTube about characters linked to products (such as the leprechaun of Lucky Charms cereal)
- Twitter or Facebook posts "from" television shows or movies that promote advertisers' products

Ads aren't all bad. They can provide people with useful information. However, you should be aware of the tricks advertisers use to catch your attention. Part of being a smart spender is knowing when someone is trying to sell you something.

CHAPTER TWO

Why Smart Spending Matters

· ·

What if you could buy anything you wanted, whenever you wanted it, and never had to ask how much it cost? That sounds great. Sadly, though, most people will never be billionaires.

No matter how successful you become, chances are that you will not be a billionaire, either. Like most people, you will have a limited amount of money to spend. Whether you have $5 or $5 million, you can learn to use it well.

Going on a spending spree can be fun, but you can't do it every day.

Getting Started Early

It's never too soon to begin gaining **financial** knowledge. This simply means knowing about money and how to manage it. That's because the habits people learn when they are young can stick around throughout their whole lives. If you want to be money-smart when you are older, start now.

Every time you spend money, you make a choice. You are deciding how to use your money. You are also deciding how not to use it, because money can only be spent once. Kids and adults both have to make decisions about money. As you'll see in this chapter, every money decision has consequences, or things that happen because of the choices that were made.

Paying a High Price

One common money mistake is overpaying for something, which means paying more than it is worth, or more than you might have paid for the same thing if you had bought it somewhere else.

For example, suppose there is a new video game you cannot wait to play. The very first time you see it for sale online or in a store, you buy it. The price is $40 dollars, which is just about all the money you have saved, but now you have that new game! Now imagine that a few days later you see the game for sale in a different store for $35 dollars, five less than you paid. A month after that, at the same place you bought the game, the price drops to $32 dollars, eight less than you paid!

You might feel that you overpaid for the game. If you had looked for it at more than one store, or waited a few weeks to buy it, you could have saved five or even eight dollars that you could have used for something else. You would be well on your way to your next purchase.

The same thing can happen with much bigger purchases, such as buying a car, but overpaying for a car could cost the buyer thousands of dollars, not just five or eight.

"Oops! I Spent It All"

Having money to spend on things you want can be a great feeling. Maybe you've been looking forward to seeing a new movie. While you're at the movie, you want something to drink and a large popcorn, and maybe some

If adults do not make good spending decisions, they may run into real trouble when they cannot pay their bills.

candy. It all adds up. In one night you could spend fifteen dollars or more.

What if that's all the money you had? Maybe you'll get by just fine with no money until next week, when you get your allowance. Maybe something will come up sooner, though, and you'll have to buy a present for a friend's birthday or you'll really want a new shirt you've seen on sale. You may wish you hadn't spent everything on that one night at the movies.

Adults can have the same problem if they spend all their money right away. Unexpected things happen. Car tires go flat and have to be replaced, or washing machines break and need to be fixed. If all the money has been spent, people have none left for emergencies, or to pay their bills. Smart spending means knowing how to budget your money so that you can pay for what you need.

Borrowers, Banks, and Credit Cards

To make a big purchase, such as a car or a house, most people have to borrow money. This is called taking out a loan.

Usually, when people take out a loan they borrow the money from a bank. The bank becomes a lender, lending money to a borrower. Not everyone can take out a loan. Banks want to know certain things about the people who ask to borrow money. Has the person borrowed money before? If so, was the loan paid back? How does the person plan to use the loan?

If a bank decides to lend money, the bank and the borrower sign a contract spelling out how and when the borrower will repay the loan. The borrower

will have to pay back more than the amount of the loan. The additional money is called **interest**. It is what the bank gets in return for making the loan.

Credit cards work the same way. People can use credit cards to buy things, but they are really borrowing that money from the credit card company. Unless they pay the whole amount back to the credit card company that same month, they will have to pay interest every month until they have repaid the entire amount.

Taking out a loan is sometimes a good thing. It may be the only way to make a needed purchase. Borrowers should always be sure, however, that they know the true cost of the loan.

CHAPTER THREE

The Math of Money

....

Being a smart spender involves some simple arithmetic. You probably already have the mathematical skills you need to help you make the most of your spending money. A shopping trip is a good way to practice those skills.

Grocery Shopping by the Numbers

You probably do not buy groceries for your family, but do you go along to the store? The next time you are in a supermarket, you can sharpen your spending skills, and maybe help with the grocery shopping.

Every trip to the grocery store is a great opportunity to learn and practice smart-spending basics.

Your first opportunity to be a smart spender comes before you even set foot in the store. Start by knowing how much money you are likely to spend. Here's how one family of three people did the math. They kept a record of all of their grocery purchases for each week, then added four weeks together to see how much they spent in a month:

Week 1	$176
Week 2	$110
Week 3	$ 89
+Week 4	$153
Total	**$528**

The family spent a total of $528 on groceries during the month. When they divided $528 by 4 (the number of weeks in the month), they learned that they spent an average of $132 on groceries each week:

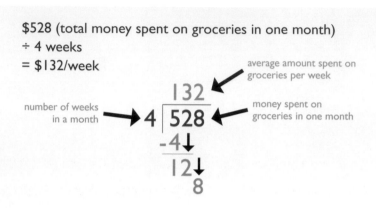

$528 (total money spent on groceries in one month)
÷ 4 weeks
= $132/week

average amount spent on groceries per week

number of weeks in a month

money spent on groceries in one month

The family decided they could save a little money by cutting back on some extras, such as potato chips. They agreed to make $125 their limit for each week's grocery shopping. They made a game of smarter shopping. If they managed to buy what they needed for less than $125, they saved the extra money for a visit to a water park.

Compare Prices

Comparing grocery prices is another way to practice smart spending. In most supermarkets, every item has a label on the shelf. The label gives the **unit price** of the item. This is the total price of the item divided by the number of units, such as ounces or pounds, in the item.

Unit prices make it easy to compare the costs of different products. For example, a 60-ounce package

Compare the unit price (in red) to find the best buy.

of ice cream has a total price of $5.40. When $5.40 is divided by 60, the price of one ounce of the ice cream turns out to be 9 cents, which is less than 10 cents.

A smaller package of the same ice cream might have a lower total price but a higher unit price, because each ounce costs more. By comparing the unit prices of different-sized packages or different brands of ice cream, customers can find the ice cream with the lowest price per ounce.

$5.40 = 540¢
540¢ ÷ 60 oz
9¢/oz, or $0.09/oz

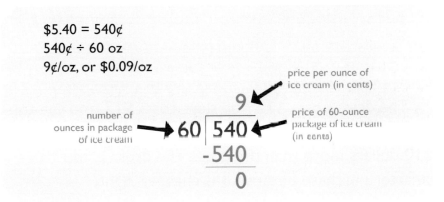

Shopping for Clothes

A little simple math can also help with smart spending on clothes. For example, suppose a girl is looking for a new dress when she sees a skirt and top that she also likes. She can only buy one new outfit. Should she buy the dress, or the skirt and top?

What Are Those Black Lines?

Most things for sale in stores have **bar codes**, also called **Universal Product Codes**, or UPCs, on their labels. These sets of closely spaced black lines are code for the long strings of numbers that identify every product in the store. When you buy something, the store employee uses a special machine called a scanner to read the UPC on the item. UPCs came into use starting in the 1970s because they are easy for scanners to read.

The dress costs $22. The skirt costs $17, and the top costs $15. Together, the skirt and top cost $32— $10 dollars more than the dress. The dress is the smarter purchase because it is cheaper, right?

Skirt	$17	**Outfit**	$32
+ Top	$15	**- Dress**	$22
Outfit	**$32**	**Difference**	**$10**

Before you buy a pair of jeans, think about how often you will wear them. Basic styles are usually a smarter buy than super trendy ones.

Not necessarily. A dress is one outfit. So is the new skirt and top. But suppose the girl already has two skirts and two pairs of pants that she could wear with the new top—that's four more outfits. If she also has three tops that she could wear with the new skirt, that's another three outfits. By spending $10 more, she gets a total of eight outfits, not just one.

Another smart-spending tip is to ask yourself how often you will wear or use something. A boy shopping for clothes, for example, might notice that one jacket that is well made, with good material, costs more than the other jackets on the rack. Will it last longer than one made of flimsy material, with loose threads? Is he likely to wear it much more often? If the answer is "yes," he might save money in the long run by buying the more expensive jacket. In other words, sometimes it's smart to spend more.

Fight That Impulse!

Have you noticed that supermarkets often put candy bars and magazines in the checkout lines, where people wait to pay for their groceries? The stores want people to make impulse buys. An impulse is a sudden, unplanned urge, and stores have learned that people waiting in line sometimes give in to impulses. They may buy a small, colorful item that was not on their shopping list if it is right in front of them.

CHAPTER FOUR

To Spend or Not to Spend?

·····································

Making good decisions about money means weighing the good and the bad aspects of spending. Like everything else in life, smart spending has disadvantages and advantages. Your goal is to find a balance between the two.

Making Difficult Decisions

Being a smart spender means that you will not always be able to buy whatever you want, when you want it. That can be disappointing, especially if your friends are buying or doing things that you cannot afford because you have decided to use your money differently.

23

Do Kids Spend or Save?

A 2012 study looked at how young people used their allowances. According to the study, only 1 percent of kids save anything from their allowances. Most kids spend it all. They use their money to buy games, toys, and clothes, but most of it gets spent on food and entertainment when they are hanging out with friends.

Sometimes the smart spending choice is the practical choice, even if it seems like less fun. For example, suppose you have saved $75. Your goal is to buy a bicycle so that you can deliver newspapers to make some extra money. With a paper route, you would earn $8 each week. You need $20 more to buy the bicycle, which costs $95.

You are on your way to your goal, but then your friend shows you a cool new hand-held game console that costs $72. Your first thought is, "I want it, and I have enough money to buy it!" You get excited about buying the console, until you remember your plan to buy the bicycle.

Saving your money until you can buy the bicycle will give you the opportunity to make more money. Spending it on the game console would give you the fun of playing with a new gadget and showing it to your friends.

Video game or bike—which do you think is the smarter way to spend? Try looking at the long-term picture.

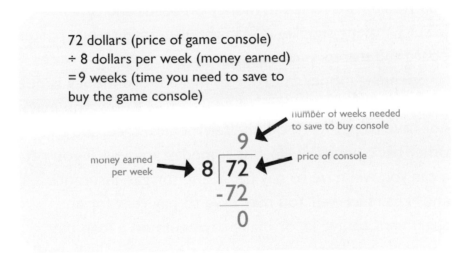

72 dollars (price of game console)
÷ 8 dollars per week (money earned)
= 9 weeks (time you need to save to buy the game console)

number of weeks needed to save to buy console

money earned per week

price of console

$$8 \overline{)72} \atop \begin{array}{r} 9 \\ \hline 72 \\ -72 \\ \hline 0 \end{array}$$

However, you would also have to start again to save for the bicycle. That would push the paper route and the money you could earn much further away.

Which is the smarter spending choice? The bicycle is the smarter choice, because you could use it to earn money, and for fun, too. Once you have the bicycle and the paper route, you could earn enough from the paper route to buy the console in nine weeks if you still want it.

Smart spending isn't always easy. Choosing not to buy something can be painful. Only you can tell if the reward is worth it.

Reasons to Spend

The choice between a bicycle and a game console shows how spending money (on the bicycle) can sometimes help you make more money (with the paper route). The same thing might happen if you and a friend decided to start a business making and selling bead jewelry. You would have to spend money on beads and other jewelry-making supplies. You might also need to buy poster board and markers to make signs advertising your wares.

Spending money in order to make more money is not the only reason to spend, of course. Right now, you may not have to pay for food, shelter, medical care, and the other basic needs of life, but someday you will. If you get a car, you will have to pay for it, and for gas, insurance, and repairs as well. You may have to pay rent for an apartment to live in, or make payments on a loan that you took out from a bank to buy a house. You will need to buy groceries and pay for health insurance. Smart spending is all about using money well so that there is enough for the basics, and some extras, too.

Share the Wealth

One way to spend money is sharing. Many people bring happiness to others and themselves through giving. This might mean buying the perfect birthday gift for a friend, or holiday presents for family members. It could also mean donating money to a charity or cause that you believe in. All of these can be part of an overall spending plan.

Giving gifts can be one of the most rewarding ways to spend money. Donating to a worthy cause is another.

As you start making bigger spending decisions, you might want to open up a bank account. This can help you save for large purchases.

Finally, don't overlook the importance of fun. A good spending plan leaves room for some pleasures, such as buying a new game, seeing a movie, or doing something enjoyable with friends. People who never give themselves such things are missing out on part of life.

The key is choosing when to treat yourself. It should be a decision, not a habit. You will probably never be able to buy or do everything you want, at least not right away, or all at once. You will have many opportunities to spend money on things you enjoy, though. Smart spending will keep fun in your financial future.

CHAPTER FIVE

Using Money Wisely

. . . .

Anyone who wants to be a smart spender has many ways to achieve that goal. This chapter explains some of the tips and tools that people use to get the most out of their money.

Do Your Research

Imagine that a college student named Nick has to buy a new computer to use in school. The job of being a smart spender starts before Nick even sets foot in a store.

Nick's first task is to figure out how much he can afford to spend, or wants to spend. He has saved some money from Christmas and birthday gifts, and he also earns money with a part-time job. He decides he can spend $800 on the new computer. Now he can start looking at computers in his **price range**, $800 or less.

Instead of going to a store and buying the first $800 computer he sees, Nick gathers information. He searches in recent issues of computer magazines online or at the library for articles with titles like "Best Computers Under $800" or "Top Choices for Student Computers." He visits several stores so he can get hands-on experience with several computers in his price range.

Nick narrows his choice to one, two, or three computer models that meet his needs. Now it is time for him to start shopping.

Online Reviews: Read with Care

Search the Internet for almost any product, and you will find reviews posted by people who have bought or used it. These are called user reviews or customer reviews. They can be helpful, if you know how to read them. Comments such as "Terrible product!" or "I love this product!" are useless. Look for reviews that give details about exactly what the user hated or loved. Also, look for reviews that compare the product with other products like it.

Going to a mall is one of the easiest ways to compare prices. You can check out several stores and find out which one has the best deal just by walking around.

Find the Best Deals

Smart spenders want to pay the lowest possible price for what they buy. The best way to do this is by **comparison shopping**. This means looking for the desired product in several places, both in stores and online, to find the best price. If the lowest price is offered by an online store, be sure to find out whether there will be an additional shipping charge. That will increase the overall cost.

Sales and coupons are good ways to save money on large purchases, such as cars and computers, and small ones, such as groceries and games. Coupons can often be found in newspapers or on stores' websites. Department stores and other businesses advertise sales, which are times when prices for some goods are lowered. Often it makes sense to put off making a purchase until the item is on sale.

Checking prices online can give you an idea of how much something costs without leaving your house.

Think Ahead

Nick has found the right computer at the best price. However, he has a few more questions to ask before he buys it. He wants to know about the **warranty** and the return policy.

A warranty tells what the seller or manufacturer of a product will do to help the customer if a product turns out to be broken or has some other problem. Will the manufacturer replace Nick's computer, or repair it? How long will the computer be covered by the warranty? If the warranty is for one year, Nick might decide to pay a little extra money to buy an extended warranty that would protect his computer for a longer period of time.

Keep That Paperwork

When you buy something, the store or restaurant gives you a **receipt** that shows what you bought, when you bought it, and how much it cost. Most receipts are small strips of paper, but if you have an email address, you might be asked if you want the receipt emailed to you. Make a habit of keeping your receipts, at least for a month or so. If you want to return a purchase to the store, you will probably need to bring the receipt.

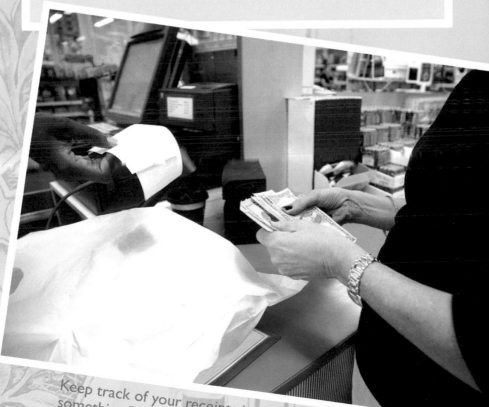

Keep track of your receipts in case you need to return something. They also help you track your spending.

The return policy is the seller's rule for taking back merchandise that the customer has decided not to keep. Some stores give the customer back the money that was paid for the merchandise. Others give the customer credit that must be used to buy something else in the same store. Some stores may not accept returns at all. Like warranties, returns usually have a time limit.

Finally, smart spenders think about future costs, such as care and maintenance, before making a purchase. A game, toy, or book may not come with any future costs. What about a dress or coat that has to be dry-cleaned, or a car that requires gas, insurance, and maintenance? A pet will need food and veterinary care. Using money wisely means thinking about what things will cost not just the day you buy them, but for as long as you own them.

If you want to buy a turtle, be sure to budget for a tank and food.

CHAPTER SIX

Become a Smart Spender

N ow that you know why smart spending is a good idea, and you have learned about some of the tips and tools that smart spenders use, it's time to make smart spending part of your life. Start by taking three important steps.

Step One: Track Your Spending

Before you can spend smarter, you need to know your own spending habits. The best way to see how you are now spending money is to track every penny.

SPENDING TRACKER

Clothing			Transportation			Personal Care		
Date	$$	Item	Date	$$	Item	Date	$$	Item

This kind of spending tracker lets you list everything you spend by the type of expense. Before you buy, ask yourself if the purchase is a want or a need. If the expense is a want, will it prevent you from buying something you need?

You can track your spending on a sheet of paper or in a special notebook that you set aside for the purpose. If you would rather use a computer or smartphone, you might find an "expense tracker" app that works. All you really need, though, is a simple chart like this:

Date	Amount	Type of Expense
September 3	$7	Movie
September 5	95¢	Candy bar
September 5	$12	Sneakers (Mom paid half)

Food			Entertainment			Other		
Date	$$	Item	Date	$$	Item	Date	$$	Item

Track your expenses for at least a month. In fact, it's a good idea to keep doing it. Many people find that the simple act of writing down what they spend makes them smarter about money.

Step Two: Look at the Big Picture

Once you have tracked your spending for a month or so, you can review it and answer two questions: "How much money do I spend?" and "Where does my money go?"

For example, you might find that you spend nearly all of your money on entertainment, such as movies and concerts. Maybe a lot of your money goes toward

Act Like a
Millionaire

When millionaires were interviewed about their financial habits, there were some surprises. Not all rich people are big, flashy spenders. Many millionaires buy used cars and shop with coupons. One habit that many of them share is keeping careful track of everything they spend. To do things like a millionaire, get started now with a spending journal of your own, and make it a habit.

building your collection of action figures or necklaces. Perhaps you will discover that you are spending half your money on fast food. Do you see patterns in your spending? Are they what you expected? Can you think of ways to change them?

For each item on your spending list, ask yourself, "Did I *need* this, or did I *want* it?" If you find a pattern in your spending, you might be able to predict how you will spend money in the future. You can also decide whether or not you should shift your spending from the wants you have to the needs. When people determine what they will spend ahead of time, they create a budget.

Tracking how you use your money now will help you make smart spending decisions in the future.

Budgets are a great way to make sure you stick to smart spending habits.

Spending money on things just because you want them is fine—as long as you leave some for what you need. Suppose your school backpack is falling apart, for example. You will need a new one for next year. If you start setting aside a little money each week, by the time you have to buy that backpack you will have enough money to get a good one. Think of the money you set aside now as "future spending."

Step Three: Set Spending Goals

Finally, make a list of your spending goals. Be specific. Here are examples of some goals:

- $48 for new backpack by July
- $10 for movie with friends once a month

Is There Another Way?

Smart spenders look for ways to get what they want without spending a lot. For example, it's exciting to see a brand new movie, but if you can manage to wait a few weeks or a month, you might be able to see it at a cheaper theater. In the meantime, many libraries have collections of movies and music that you can borrow for free.

- $4 for treats each week
- $700 for a tablet by seventh grade

Some of your goals will guide your spending for things you need and want now. If you have goals for the future, though, you will need to start setting money aside for them. A good spending plan includes saving money. You might decide to save a certain amount, such as five or ten dollars, every month. You could also decide to save one-third of all the money you receive. Either way, do not think of saving money as taking money away from what you could be buying right now. Think of it as a different kind of spending—giving money to yourself in the future.

Being responsible about spending can be both efficient and fun. Smart decisions let you make the most of what you have to spend.

Whatever your spending habits and goals, following these three steps will mean that when you do spend your money, you'll have the satisfaction of knowing that you spent it well and wisely.

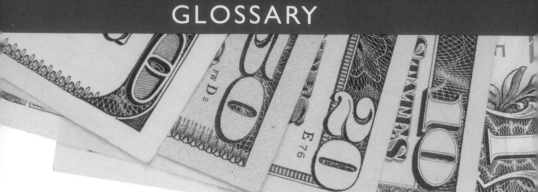

advertising The use of messages called advertisements (ads) to call people's attention to something and influence them to buy a product, use a service, or support a political candidate.

bank A business that serves as a place where people can store their money and that also lends money in the form of loans, charging interest on the loans to those who borrow money.

bar code A row of black lines that is code for the specific number used to identify a product in a store; also called a Universal Product Code.

barter The exchange or trade of goods or services for other goods or services.

bill Paper money, or a statement of money that is owed.

coin A unit of money usually made of metal.

comparison shopping Looking for the same item at different stores to find which store has the lowest price.

consumer Someone who buys a product or uses a service.

currency Anything that the people in a particular country or region agree to use as money.

financial Having to do with money.

interest Money that is added to the amount of a loan; the borrower must repay the original loan plus the interest.

loan Money that is borrowed and must be repaid over time, usually with interest.

money Currency with a set value that can be exchanged for goods or services, or used to pay bills. Usually created and managed by the government.

price range The highest and lowest amounts that someone is able or willing to spend for a specific product.

psychology The study of the mind and how it works.

receipt The paper or digital record of a purchase that is given to someone who buys an object or pays for a service.

sponsor The person, company, or group that pays for an ad.

unit price The cost of a given amount of something; for example, many things sold in grocery stores have price labels showing the unit price per ounce, so that people can compare the costs of different brands and sizes.

Universal Product Code (UPC) Another name for a bar code.

warranty An agreement that spells out a seller's or manufacturer's responsibility for a product; the warranty says what the seller or manufacturer will do if there is something wrong with the product, and for how long.

Books

Furgang, Kathy. *National Geographic Kids Everything Money: A wealth of facts, photos, and fun!* Des Moines, IA: National Geographic Children's Books, 2013.

Nourigat, Paul. *Spending Success.* Portland, OR: FarBeyond Publishing, 2012.

Reynolds, Mattie. *Super Smart Shopping.* South Egremont, MA: Red Chair Press, 2013.

Websites

Financial Entertainment

financialentertainment.org
This library of free games that can be played online or on mobile devices teaches kid about making money-related decisions. The game Celebrity Calamity focuses on spending and credit cards.

The Mint: Fun for Kids

themint.org/kids
This site, sponsored by a financial company, offers games and quizzes for kids on the subjects of earning, saving, and spending.

Spending Smarts: Think Before You Buy

pbskids.org/itsmylife/money/spendingsmarts
This PBS site gives kids advice about smart spending, along with tools such as a printable journal for recording their spending decisions.

INDEX

Rebecca Stefoff has written books for young readers on many topics. She is the author of the six-volume series Is It Science? (Cavendish Square, 2014), and the four-volume series Animal Behavior Revealed (Cavendish Square, 2014). *Smart Spending* is her first book about finance, and she wishes that she had learned about managing money when she was a kid. You can learn more about Stefoff and her books for young people at rebeccastefoff.com.